summoned at every age

THE IGNATIAN IMPULSE SERIES

summoned at every age

finding God

in our

later years

Peter van Breemen, S.J.

ave maria press AmP Notre Dame, Indiana

First published as *Alt werden als geistlicher Weg* in Germany in 2004 by Echter Verlag.

© 2005 Ave Maria Press, Inc.

www.avemariapress.com

International Standard Book Number: 1-59471-036-8

Cover and text design by Brian C. Conley

Printed and bound in the United States of America.

Library of Congress Cataloging-in-Publication Data is available.

C O N T E N T S

PREFACE

Aging is a gift. But if it is a gift, it is also a task: a multifaceted and complex task. In offering these reflections on the spiritual dimension of getting older, I am drawing on my own experience, and my years of reflection on it. Born in 1927, I am a fellow traveler on path of aging and its spiritual effects. And because I have been a Jesuit since 1945, all that follows is rooted in Ignatian spirituality.

I have discussed the topic of aging with many friends and acquaintances, sometimes with this book in mind. Therefore I would like to take this opportunity to express my deepest gratitude to the following people for their contributions: Hans I. Oudshoorn, S.J., who tended to his fellow Jesuits at the Berchmanianum, the Jesuits' retirement and long term care facility in Nymwegen, Holland, for many years; Sophie Montaperto, who cared for the aged at a Bavarian retirement home and extended care facility for many years; and Sr. Ignatia Bentele, who shared with me much insight based on her long-time experience and advanced age. I sincerely thank all of them and the many other people whom I am unable to mention here by name.

I owe most of my thoughts and insights to my fellow Jesuits at the Peter-Faber-Kolleg retirement home in Berlin-Kladow. I spent close to nine years in their company. This was a precious, albeit not always easy, time; but I did gather from them a lot of knowledge on the topics addressed in this little book. Eight years ago, I published an article on the topic of "A Spirituality of Aging." This essay was based on my experiences with my fellow priests. Most of them have since come to the end of their journey on earth. I remember them here in my heart with warmth and gratitude.

My hope is that this small book will help many people experience harmony and fruitfulness during the sometimes difficult final stage of their lives.

PETER VAN BREEMEN, S.J.
AACHEN, GERMANY

C HAPTER ONE

LIFE SUMMONS US AT EVERY AGE

One cannot spend the evening of one's life in the same way that one has spent the morning, even though morning and evening are so essentially connected that they cannot be separated on an experiential level. Although they all are only different phases of the one life that is reaching for completeness, what was very important at the beginning can turn out to be rather insignificant toward the end, and something that had initially played a small role can become completely dominant in the final stage. This same paradox of unity being comprised of diverse and distinct parts is well illustrated by our own bodies: just as our body replaces all its cells every seven years while still, and in spite of this process, remaining distinctly *our* body, the different stages of the development of our personality shape the growth of one's *unique* life. At the same time, each individual stage of life possesses not only its own task and transformation, its own beauty and charm, but also its very own dangers and pitfalls. Overall, even in its final phase, human existence is perhaps above all *one* lifelong learning process.

In a poem, entitled "Stages of Life," the German poet, Hermann Hesse (1877–1962), describes his own vivid experience of this connection in the following way:

Stages of Life
As every flower fades and as all youth
departs, so life at every stage,
so every virtue, so our grasp of truth,
blooms in its day and may not last forever.

Since life may summon us at every age,
be ready, heart, for parting, new endeavor,
be ready bravely and without remorseto find new
light that old ties cannot give.
In all beginnings dwells a magic force
for guarding us and helping us to live.
Serenely let us move to distant places
and let no sentiments of home detain us.
The Cosmic Spirit seeks not to restrain us
but lifts us stage by stage to wider spaces.
If we accept a home of our own making,
familiar habit makes for indolence.
We must prepare for parting and leave-taking
or else remain the slaves of permanence.
Even the hour of our death may send
us speeding on to fresh and newer spaces,
and life may summon us to newer races.
So be it, heart: bid farewell without end.
                                        —HERMAN HESSE

The more advanced our life, the more clearly life reveals its basic structures. At times, in old age, insights will surface that could not be noticed when we were completely absorbed by our activities; once grasped, the insights begin shedding light on earlier stages of our lives. Thus, the psalmist is able to pray: "So teach us to count our days that we may gain a wise heart" (Ps 90:12).

This natural interrelationship between the different phases of life suggests that the spiritual aspects of aging can normally be noticed most readily by a person whose life up to that point was spiritually active, or at least touched by a sense of spirituality. If the spiritual life has not begun during one's active, pre-senescent life, it will be more difficult for it to take hold during old age. Many a person fails to make this discovery until it is too late, leaving him or her bitterly disappointed. However, it should be added at once that grace is capable of always creating what our rules fail to accomplish, no matter how smart and clever they may be.

As we age we make room for values that were important and precious throughout our lives, but which were sometimes given little opportunity to develop. For instance:

- To practice silence and seek conscious contact with the source of our being;
- To stop being busy in order to be able to listen quietly to those close to us;
- To rid ourselves of unholy or even holy compulsions;
- To set out on that inner journey that Dag Hammerskjöld (1905–1961) liked to call the longest journey of all. Dag Hammerskjöld was secretary-general of the United Nations from 1953 to 1961 and Nobel Peace Prize winner (awarded posthumously) in 1961.
- To let important recollections and memories surface and, subsequently, quietly enjoy them.

The price for these gains is frequently high. Physical as well as mental strength and ability decrease with age, while frailty and illness increase. What this means is that we will depend more and more on the help of others. This requires and promotes a process of maturity that can take place only if we accept the fact that our strength is dwindling. We are constantly tempted to act "as if"—as if we were still able to do a lot of things, as if we still had a lot of this or that, as if our situation were not all that bad. It takes honesty and humility to genuinely admit that we are aging and then to accept it. But once we do, advanced age can turn into a time of enrichment and grace. Many an aging person has come to this awareness and, in doing so, has in turn enriched the lives of many others.

Here, too, a law of life repeats itself. Whatever we truly are will always depend on three factors: First, there is the hereditary makeup that our genes predetermine. They predetermine if we are going to be male or female, the color of our skin and our hair, our body type, and many additional features. All this is pre-established. The second factor is another set of givens: our social environment and the events of our life's history that "just happen." The interaction of these social factors with our hereditary factors create what can be referred to as our natural makeup. They provide the slate on which we write the story of our lives. This ability to write our own story is the third factor. It is the gift of human freedom: the leeway given us in choosing our actions. While in a certain set of circumstances one person may become resigned and stagnant, another will see them as an opportunity for improvement and growth. While one person may interpret a negative event as an assault on his or her personality or as a form of personal defeat, another person will sense it as a challenge.

Admittedly, many things in our lives cannot be changed; still, the crucial question will always remain how we will deal with these immutable things. There are some situations that are not subject to change, but our responses to them can be altered. And it is here that we encounter an influence that can turn out to be substantial. C.G. Jung expressed this as follows: "Only what one accepts can be changed." Whatever one refuses to accept can no longer be influenced. However, if we accept it, we may be able to change it into something good and beneficial. This does not only apply to things and situations. What is even more important is the fact that it applies also to human beings. The older we get the more important this law of life becomes.

Not everything that happens is necessarily determined by God's will. I am convinced that there are some events and deeds that are not willed by God. For instance, blaming the will of God for a traffic death caused by a drunk driver would be a gross oversimplification. Driving under the influence is certainly not God's will. However, even in such circumstances God wants "that all things work together for good for those who love" him (Rom 8:28). In order to accomplish this, God normally requires our cooperation. God acts through human beings. Thus the issue is how we will be able to turn events that "just happen" into something good by cooperating with God.

Initially, what matters is how we perceive the facts in relation to God and how we approach them. God's dealings with us do not swoop down on us like a kind of fate to which we must subject ourselves. This would lead to a fatalistic view of life contrary to Christian thinking. Leading a Christian life is indeed an art. It requires a balanced perspective on the relationship between the so-called facts and the presence and action of God. According to Ignatius' description in the *Spiritual Exercises*, God "works for me in all the creatures on the face of the earth; that is, he acts in the manner of one who is laboring" (SE 236).

On November 17, 1944, despite being imprisoned in Berlin-Tegel with both his hands shackled, a Jesuit priest named Alfred Delp, wrote:

> *One thing is both clear and has felt unlike anything else: the world is ever so full of God. From the pores of every living thing he seemingly reaches out to us. Yet, we frequently turn a blind eye to him. We become stuck in both beautiful and bad moments, failing to experience them, even to the point where they emanate from God. This applies to everything beautiful as well as everything miserable. God wants to celebrate our encounter with him in everything, questioning us and putting us to the test, while waiting for our worship and dedication.*

Even during this darkest of hours, Alfred Delp was searching for a worshipful reply and devotion in response to an encounter with God. No doubt, he must have learned this from the founder of his order: always cooperate with God as best as you can, always be an instrument in the hands of God, and, together with God, always work towards turning everything to good.

In the eyes of St. Ignatius, the task that Christ entrusts to us lasts throughout our entire lives. Several years ago, the Jesuit provincial for California caused quite a stir when he insisted that Jesuits know no retirement. Interpreting his comments to mean that all Jesuits must work until their dying days misses the point. Rather, what he meant was that Jesuits never retire from their mission, or, to put it differently, even retirement is part of a Jesuit's task and mission. Although the latter formulation dispels any misunderstanding, it also removes the provocative nature of the statement. Even when our strength weakens and we are no longer capable of physical work, the mission stands as stated. Ignatius included even death in this mission. In the Constitutions, the founder of the Jesuit order writes: "As they have done throughout their lives, every member of the Society of Jesus must make every effort, even more so in the hour of his death, both to honor and serve God, our Lord, and to assure that our fellow human beings will be edified, at least by the example of his patience and courage together with the living faith, hope, and love for the eternal benefits Christ, our Lord, has earned and obtained by the incomparable hardships of his temporal life and death."

While Ignatius intended this mission statement in the Constitutions for his fellow Jesuits, it is essentially applicable to every Christian. For the life of everybody who has been baptized is characterized by a mission that encompasses his or her entire life. In spite of advanced age, even older Christians keep serving the kingdom of God, regardless of the specific nature of their service. That is why the gospel assigns a precious value to old age. This is quite some present handed to us as part of the good news of the gospel. It encourages us to accept the hardships and setbacks of old age patiently and without self-pity, because the hardships can be seen within the greater context.

When I discussed my intentions of writing this book with an eighty-nine-year-old woman and mentioned the word "task" in relationship to aging, she responded spontaneously: "But getting old is not only a task, it is above all a gift." She is right. One cannot separate gift from task. And it is a good idea to emphasize the gift, for this will help us to be diligent in completing the task.

STAGE BY STAGE TO WIDER SPACES

When we reflect on the process of aging it is help-ful to remember that it occurs in several stages. As the number of "seniors" in our society grows ever larger, both numerically and in terms of their percent-age of the population, they are also becoming more and more differentiated. At first glance, one can imme-diately distinguish among:

- The so-called "young seniors," i.e. people who just joined the ranks of the retired and who have remained both mentally and physically fit;
- People who are fading fast;
- People in need of assistance;
- People who suffer from personality-altering ill-nesses, such as senility, dementia, and Alzheimer's disease.

Within these groupings there are many differences. Financially, even among older people, the disparity between the rich and the poor is apparent and it is on the rise. There are likewise great differences in their cultural and intellectual backgrounds. As a result, the quality of life during this time varies greatly.

Many in the first group of so-called young seniors have discovered ways to take advantage of their newly gained freedom and leisure. They are the envy of many as a result and are even occasionally caricatured. They are in a position to do things they had looked forward to all along, and they do not hesitate to seize the opportunity. Some pursue educational opportunities, taking advantage of courses of study specifically tailored to them by universities. These courses aim to foster greater insight rather than a mere accumulation of facts and figures. They often make an important contribution to the happiness and fulfillment that many seniors experience. Free of the pressure of having to work for a living, many seniors offer their experience and skills to others. For instance, I know of a fellow Jesuit who had previously taught at a prep school and now uses part of his free time to teach German to refugees, an activity that keeps him young and cheerful. In a large city, a computer specialist drops by the office of Catholic Charities on a weekly basis for an entire afternoon in order to help solve difficult computer problems. No doubt most of us are familiar with similarly inspiring examples of people who share gratefully and happily some of the gifts they have acquired during their active lives.

In many parts of the world, young people have the opportunity to become involved in social work under the guidance of a Jesuit. There is, for example, a program called the Jesuit Volunteer Corps. For a year, sometimes two years, young adults share living quarters in small, mixed groups, purposefully adopting a simple lifestyle. Everybody works in some manner for a marginalized group or the socially disadvantaged. Their communal life leaves room for times of prayer and spiritual exchange and, once a year, they participate in individual retreats lasting eight days. Similar groups for "young seniors" have arisen for a couple years now, calling themselves Ignatian Lay Volunteer Corps. Many older people appreciate this combination of spiritual community life and social engagement as a welcome transition from their work lives to retirement.

The challenge facing the second group of seniors, those whose mental and physical health is steadily diminishing, is entirely different. They are painfully aware of their fading memories, especially their increased inability to recall names and facts. Additionally, they notice their diminishing hearing and vision, leading to ever increasing isolation. They are still able to do many things on their own, but it is an unusually slow, taxing process, withering their own and others' patience. The frailty of old age overwhelms them and confronts them with the difficult task of learning to cope with it. Above all, these people must learn to come to terms with their limitations. In a world idealizing what is taller, faster, and more plentiful, their age forces them to move in the opposite direction. Their physical strength, their ability to concentrate, and their endurance are waning. The standards by which they used to measure their lives are now losing their validity and applicability, which requires a difficult adjustment. They must set aside these old standards and accept new measures for all things. Wise people manage to peg their own measures and adjust their lives accordingly, even when faced by the inevitability of fading strength.

While Ignatius always considered the *magis*, i.e. the striving for "more" and greater things, as an ideal, he also defined it as *discreta caritas*, discrete, discerning love. This open-ended use of the comparative is characteristic of Ignatius' thinking. In our youth, many among us used to write at the top of our exams and homework the motto AMDG, *Ad Majorem Dei Gloriam*: not for the *greatest* glory of God, but, using the comparative, for the *greater* glory of God. Truly this sense of more or the greater is a dynamic ideal that shapes our journey toward God, the one who is always greater, in the process transforming us into lifelong pilgrims. Yet this striving for more is always confronted by the need for moderation. While the need for limits and discretion stems from our personality, its foundations are rooted not in us but in the will of God. Ignatius tried to consistently discern what it is that God's will demands of us.

> *Observing moderation is not only necessary when doing what is necessary, but also when doing what is pious, so that our efforts will be able to last. This would be impossible if our efforts were immoderate. And as far as temporal events are concerned, it would be wise to prepare our hearts to accept readily from the hands of God one or the other variation, i.e. the happy as well as the untoward one. (Excerpted from a letter Ignatius wrote six months prior to his death to Girolamo Vignes)*

Over a period of time, the loss of strength may lead to complete dependency. This is, no doubt, a heavy cross to bear. Dependency is never easy to accept. It requires us to learn how to wait, not only for simple things, but also for the most intimate forms of assistance. We are entirely at the mercy of the ways in which others do things. Loneliness increases to the point of sometimes feeling abandoned. Many a thing that previously used to make our lives meaningful all but disappears. In the eyes of others the simple presence of a sick person can be rather meaningful; yet, for the most part, the ailing person is not even aware of such a connection and is reluctant to believe that this indeed might be the case.

Events and accomplishments that used to be the basis of our self-worth—professional activity, the joy of working and being productive—now fall by the wayside. So does the concern for family and engagement on behalf of our fellow human beings. Our influence and position in life, our physical appearance and physical strength, and often even our memory, hearing, and vision decline. Confronted by this situation, we must search anew for the meaning underlying this phase of life. Happy are those who have lived a life based on faith. While the question about the meaning of life is now restated, they are able to connect it to the earlier support provided by faith. Now, the issue will be returning to the foundation that will be capable of supporting their entire life.

We live in an achievement-oriented society that determines people's worth by the level and the number of their achievements. Such is the air we breathe and the climate in which we live—a world where everything must be earned. Even during childhood we were indoctrinated in this message, absorbing it quickly. It determines our way of life. One must not only earn money and win social esteem, but also merit a good reputation and the gratitude of others, sometimes even their fidelity and affection. The gospel shows an entirely different picture. The words "performance" and "achievement" are not mentioned in the Bible. Instead, the Bible speaks frequently of fruitfulness. This calls for an entirely different attitude toward life; for fruitfulness contains a mystery that we do not comprehend. Jesus expresses this idea very beautifully and simply in the parable of the growing seed: "The kingdom of God is as if someone would scatter seed on the ground, and would sleep and rise night and day, and the seed would sprout and grow, he does not know how" (Mk 4:26–27). When it comes to performance and achievement, what truly matters is holding all the cards and having everything under control. In the kingdom of God, however, what matters is surrendering to mystery and allowing this mystery to work within us. This is the fundamental law underlying the good news and, therefore, the life of every Christian. When energy and initiative decrease during the final phase of our life, then we must live with greater devotion, relying on this fundamental attitude of faith. The faith that has been valid all along now becomes even more relevant, and the truth of faith has a liberating effect. It brings us the kind of peace that the world is incapable of giving us.

It seems to me that a life of dedication is important not only for people at an advanced age, but for everyone. It demonstrates to the world something that is grossly neglected most of the time, something that the world is in dire need of, even in church circles and Christian surroundings. This is validated by the example given by Father Pedro Arrupe, S.J. during the many years of his terminal illness. In May of 1965, he was elected Superior General of the Jesuit Order, the

Society of Jesus. He served with great dedication, guided by his deep faith and by trust. On August 7, 1981, he suffered a severe stroke at Rome's Fiumicino Airport, rendering him completely helpless. It was two years before his successor could be elected. The general congregation—a meeting of Jesuits who had gathered from all over the world to elect a new superior general—accepted Pedro Arrupe's resignation on September 3, 1983. In the afternoon of that same day, during a particularly solemn session, the following message by Pedro Arrupe was read to the assembled Jesuits: "Dear *patres*, oh how much I have wished to be able meet with you in better physical condition. As you can see, I am not even able to talk to you in person. But my assistants understood what I wanted to tell everybody individually. More than ever I am now in God's hands. This has been my fervent wish since childhood. However, now there is a difference: today, the initiative is entirely on God's side. To know and to feel that I am so completely in his hands, is truly a deep spiritual experience."

Some older people experience such a tremendous loss of strength during this phase of dependency that their personality undergoes some substantial changes. This is precisely what most people fear. More than once, people have told me how sincerely they hope and pray that they will never succumb to Alzheimer's disease or become completely paralyzed. It is difficult to appreciate the extent of the suffering experienced by these patients precisely because they are no longer able to talk about it. At the Peter-Faber-Kolleg retirement home in Berlin-Kladow, I witnessed the course that Alzheimer's disease followed in a confrere, beginning with its onset to shortly before his death. In the end, he was no longer able to verbalize anything. Yet I could tell that he still possessed all his emotions and feelings, even though he was no longer able to express them in words. At Christmas time, he surprised us all when he was capable of joining us enthusiastically in the singing of the carols.

The patient is not the only one who suffers. For the patient's loved ones, the illness is indeed a difficult cross to bear. The pain and suffering are particularly severe for a spouse when a marriage partner has succumbed to such an illness. Whenever I witness this, I am always deeply moved by the faithfulness and patience, the respect and the dedication of the healthy partner, the person who is often not completely healthy either. When it finally becomes impossible to provide care at home, the difficult but necessary decision must be made to commit the sick person to an extended care facility or nursing home. Even if this is going to provide great practical relief, it still remains a difficult, heart-rending step.

It won't take much to question—at times quite frankly—the worth of life in such a debilitated state. No matter how normal this question may be, it misses the point and reveals a worrisome fundamental attitude. Every human being possesses a dignity that cannot be measured in degrees. The worth of a life depends on a value system and is accordingly measured based on certain criteria. The worth of the life in question may vary, and at times some may say a certain life has no value. However, human dignity can never be diminished because it was God who assigned it to every human being: "God created humankind in his image" (Gn 1:27). "We do not assign human dignity to one another. That is why we cannot deny it to anyone. Human dignity is a given, it must not be violated," states Bishop Franz Kamphaus of Frankfurt, Germany. Any seriously ill person points beyond himself or herself without being aware of it. The value of this service to their fellow human beings is immeasurable.

CHAPTER THREE

OUR GIFT TO SOCIETY

The position of the elderly in our society is determined by three factors. First, the life expectancy of the population has risen considerably thanks to modern medical advances. As a result, people are not only living longer, they are also living in reasonably good health to a more advanced age. Second, as the birthrate has declined, the proportion of seniors in the population has increased. Third, the income level of some seniors has remained quite high, due not only to social security, but to other retirement plans and gains in the real estate and stock markets. Many of today's seniors are materially more independent than those in previous generations. As the retirement of the baby-boom generation approaches, there will be new strains upon the social security system and some of these advantages enjoyed today may disappear in the future.

The economy welcomes today's retirees and generates a host of senior-oriented goods for them because they are such a substantial market. There are tempting vacation offers for "young seniors," and fitness programs tailored to their needs. The food industry sees the special needs of seniors as an opportunity for sales, and insurance companies are eager to offer policies of every kind. In the political realm, seniors are recognized as an important voting bloc with considerable political power. Not only are politicians aware of their political clout, but the elderly electorate itself is conscious of its role in national and local politics, organizing themselves locally in various organizations and nationally through advocacy groups such as the AARP, the American Association of Retired Persons.

THE GIFT OF GRANDPARENTING

Grandparents frequently play a special role in families. The role of grandparents today is different from how it used to be. Grandchildren are less likely to live near their grandparents, and couples wait longer to have children. But both parents are also often working and so, if grandparents do live nearby, they are in great demand for childcare. With a lot of free time on their hands and experience under their belts, grandparents are often more relaxed than parents when dealing with their grandchildren. As an added bonus, they need not be responsible the way they used to be when raising their own children. This can only last so long though, as grandchildren eventually become so busy with activities like sports and music that they have much less time for their grandparents.

One of the most difficult challenges faced by grandparents is refraining from trying to improve the way the parents are raising their children. This would inevitably lead to an unhealthy tension in their relationship with their own children as well as their grandchildren. Occasionally, a painful, sometimes even explosive, problem exists when it comes to religion. Many grandparents are very concerned about the religious life of their children and the religious education of their grandchildren. They frequently tell me about how painful this is for them:

"They no longer attend church . . ." or "They left the church, but they are such good people. I pray for them every day." "I just can't understand." Sometimes, they blame themselves: "What have we done wrong?" They are torn between self-doubt and incomprehension, between hope and fear, all permeated by deep pain. I would like to tell these elderly: "No, you did nothing wrong." Or even better: "Of course you have made mistakes, just like everybody else raising kids. That is simply a part of bringing them up. Mistakes are part of parenting; your parents made them and your children will make them too. With so many changes happening so quickly, no method of child rearing, no preparation can adequately keep up. You've done the best you could. Now, simply entrust your situation to God. Certainly, you should pray for your children and grandchildren. I hardly need to encourage you to do so, for it stands to reason that all parents do that anyway—but trustingly, with an unencumbered heart. It would be destructive to exert pressure on your children or grandchildren. Live your life genuinely and in complete honesty. This is the best you can do for your children and grandchildren. Then God will act through you and lead everything to good."

The importance of elderly people in the life of the younger generation has changed. Nowadays, the role of grandparents in passing on knowledge and experience to a younger generation is more limited. Everything is undergoing change and developing so quickly that the knowledge of the older generation frequently lags behind. A high school teacher who is decidedly not elderly told me that he routinely turns to his students when he encounters computer problems, and gets an answer in a matter of seconds. Having grown up with the myriad new gadgets, their abilities in these areas of technology are naturally superior. But beyond technological know-how, the subject matter and abilities that younger people are expected to master is frequently rather different from that of students in the past. This makes offering direct and concrete help almost impossible. However, what seniors have to give is much more valuable than specific knowledge. It is their outlook on life and the particular perspective distilled from a lifetime of experience. Sharing this wisdom is the most significant opportunity for elders to be of authentic service to the younger generation.

Ignatius counts among the most important tasks of Jesuits that the members see to it that people who fight with one another reconcile. In the draft for the Constitutions—the so-called *Formula Instituti*, this service is expressly mentioned in the very first sentence. Frequently seniors possess a special talent in this regard. Throughout their long lives, they have likely acquired a certain gentleness and wisdom that can bear fruit in situations such as these. Older people have the time and the patience necessary to carefully reunite people who have become alienated, especially among their own relatives. Perhaps they manage to look below the surface. Both Simeon and Anna, who were highly advanced in age, could see during the presentation of Jesus in the Temple what the priests on duty and the powerful had failed to see, and they were full of joy (Lk 2:25–38). They recognized the Prince of

Peace. It could be a fitting service and a valuable help to contribute some of this peace to today's world.

READY TO RECEIVE

And yet there comes a time when the elderly are no longer capable of doing much, when they themselves are increasingly in need. Frequently, it is not easy to slip into the role of the one in need of help.

However, requiring help is part of life. This is especially obvious at the beginning of life, and also at the end. To accept help unconditionally is an important Christian value. One of the tasks that older people face is to grow in readiness to accept the necessary, proper, and realistically possible help. We must be ready to receive it from family, but also ready to recognize that they may not be able to provide us with the help we need. One of the most important lessons I have learned in this regard comes from St. Ignatius: People in need of help are a gift to the community. Ignatius always placed great value on taking care of the sick in the best way possible. He doesn't specifically mention the aged because there were hardly any among the members of the Society in his day. But his comments on sickness and death easily transfer to our situation. When he speaks of these things he is not primarily talking about the service to the sick, but rather about the service the sick perform for the healthy. The community not only needs their example, it also needs the opportunity to render assistance to the sick. They are both valuable and fruitful.

This outlook on life seems important and necessary in our times. It contains the kind of hidden truth that Jean Vanier, the founder of the l'Arche movement, has shown to be eminently fruitful. People who are commonly referred to as "handicapped" share life in l'Arche villages with people one would call "normal." However, Jean Vanier refuses to accept this distinction: In his perspective, we all have our own special handicaps and people called handicapped make an incredibly valuable contribution to the community. Before his death in 1996, the renowned Catholic writer Henry Nouwen spent the final years of his life at the l'Arche community near Toronto. In the books he wrote during his stay there he described time and again the liberating experiences he witnessed in this community, probably most poignantly in the posthumously published book *Adam, God's Beloved*. Every old person can end up facing the challenge of living one's dependency in such a way that it can become a gift to one's family and acquaintances. Let us be ready.

Occasionally, I have had the privilege to witness someone's death within the context of his or her small community or family. Sadly, this is the exception today. On one occasion, the family was able to make this possible because several daughters were nurses; in another case it was possible because the small community was attached to a nearby hospital. A Jesuit community in Bruges, Flanders also succeeded because all confreres pooled resources and had the additional benefit of outside help. In all these cases, it was a blessing for the dying person to be able to die surrounded by a familiar community. However, the death was also a deeply emotional experience for those who were able to accompany a treasured loved one on his or her final journey. They talked about it for years afterward, expressing how grateful they were that it was possible. Once again, this illustrates how Ignatius can consider illness and even death as a mutual kind of service. The hospice movement follows a similar kind of thinking with their service to the dying.

The elderly have an irreplaceable position in society, even today. We cannot genuinely exist without the presence of older people in our lives.

STIRRED TO PROFOUND GRATITUDE

Anyone who lives with a person of advanced age can undoubtedly recall numerous stories he or she has heard hundreds of times. The older people get, the greater their tendency to repeat themselves. Some are more than willing to speak, yet seldom have anything new to say. They tend instead to simply rehash what has been said previously. Initially, stories are introduced with an apology for having told them before. But soon this excuse is dropped and the storyteller is not even conscious of having told the story before. This peculiar habit of people at an advanced age reveals two contrary dangers.

On the one hand, there is the tendency to become narrowly focused, inflexible, rigid, and ritualistic. Embellishing and idealizing the past, people of advanced age cling to certain stories and use them as a means of overcoming insecurity. It is always the same old thing. The other extreme is the tendency to lose a sense of restraint, to let oneself go. This can lead to the loss of healthy boundaries between oneself and others, and to a diminished sense of orderliness. That is one reason why some older people can become unreliable and unpredictable. Loquacity is merely an symptom, a clearly perceptible sign of this danger.

One way to avoid these dangers is through involvement. The older we get the more we must take care to stay involved, keeping our minds engaged and maintaining an awareness of the present, whether it is current events, international affairs, or the state of the church. We need to stay informed as actively as possible through conversations, reading, or the media.

By these actions we promote and consciously choose the art of an overall attitude of involvement. At this stage of life, we must continue fostering cultural values, making time for inspirational reading, perhaps in the form of audio books. Another way of staying in touch and remaining alert is the through simple volunteer service that can be performed without much ado. Frequently, little acts of kindness performed out of love are of great value. Suitable hobbies, too, can be a great source of joy and vitality. As with anything else, it is important to keep an eye on what we can realistically attempt to do. Otherwise, any of these forms of involvement can end up as a negative experience.

A sense of humor is a great tool to avoid the dangers of rigidity. Humor helps us keep perspective and make connections that may otherwise be easily overlooked by the overly serious person. Humor can relax us and ease the tension of certain situations. It allows us to see things in a different light. Humor is like the sun lighting up a landscape: not a single leaf or blade of grass is different, and yet everything is so much more attractive. Humor has a way of reducing anger, annoyance, and shame. It promotes healing of injuries and offenses. People who maintain a playful attitude and can occasionally laugh at themselves are fortunate. Laughter is good for us. It physically relaxes us. Somebody once asserted that twenty seconds of laughter is the equivalent of three minutes of jogging. Besides, one can do this exercise sitting in a chair! Perhaps the most precious benefit of humor is that it helps us to see things in relative terms, that is to say, we see the proper relationship between things and assign each to its proper place and significance. In this way, we will be able to accept things more readily and integrate what life has to offer. This is precisely one of the most important tasks of old age: to accept everything, to digest and absorb everything one has experienced throughout one's life.

In the Sermon on the Mount, Jesus advises us to accept every day as it comes, one day at a time: "So do not worry about tomorrow, for tomorrow will bring worries of its own. Today's trouble is enough for today" (Mt 6:34). We must refrain from allowing ourselves to be disturbed by what might happen in the future, by what the final stages of our lives may bring in terms of illness and suffering. Sometimes people suffer most from the pain they are afraid of but which never materializes. As soon as we notice this tendency, we must consciously and resolutely counter it. Ignatius has a term for it; he calls it *agere contra*: to act against the temptation (c.f. SE 351). Thus, whenever we experience such moods and fears, we do well to simply entrust ourselves to God, to place ourselves into the hands of God, and to utter a prayer, perhaps one known by heart. Such moments of trust in God are worth their weight in gold.

Gratitude, like humor, is indispensable on the way to maturity. It dignifies and celebrates life, recognizing that life is indeed a gift. Gratitude helps us to avoid taking life and its gifts for granted or as a mere accident. Instead, it lets us trace life back to its source and acknowledge its origin. Gratitude presumes trust. We cannot be truly grateful to a person whom we do not trust, because we will be constantly plagued by an unpleasant sense that we do not know what were the real intentions behind the action.

Even more than humor, gratitude helps us integrate the various experiences of our lives. Only when we are fully grateful will we be able to completely accept life. Through gratitude, we are able to integrate and unify our lives. Then even our failures and disappointments can find a place in our lives. Then our hearts will be filled with genuine peace.

Jesus never promised that we would be spared from suffering and failure. On the contrary, Jesus clearly exhorted his disciples to accept the cross and follow him (Mt 16:24 and many other passages). From the very beginning, all Christians—above all the apostles—experienced life in all its various forms of suffering. However, they also experienced what Jesus solemnly proclaimed at the conclusion of the gospel according to St. Matthew: "And remember, I am with you always, to the end of the age" (Mt 28:20). This promise is the fulfillment of the announcement of the angel in the first chapter of the same gospel, who declared that he would be called, "Emmanuel, which means, 'God is with us'" (Mt 1:23). If we are able to faithfully accept this presence of Jesus in our lives, then we will have found the key that will enable us to accept life in its entirety. The beginning of Psalm 103 reads: "Bless the Lord, O my soul, and all that is within me, bless his holy name." Genuine maturity means that every part of us is capable of praising God, our entire person. It is at this point that every human being will experience a sense of unity and peace. Toward the end of his relatively brief life—he died when he was fifty-six—Dag Hammerskjöld wrote: "The night is closing in. For all that has been, thanks. For all that is to come, yes."

A geriatric nurse in a nursing home witnessed a woman of ninety-five who would daily sit by the window for many hours, quietly and contentedly watching people go by. One day, she asked the old lady about what occupied her so intensely. She got the following answer: "Well, you know, when I was young I never had any time to reflect on anything because I was just too busy working. But I have been living in this retirement home for eleven years now, and I must admit that I've never had it so good. I have enough to eat and a warm room of my own. That's not to be taken for granted. Most of the people working here, with a few exceptions, are attentive and friendly, and I am content. No two people are ever the same. Now, just look at nature. Hasn't God done a marvelous job? He created the animals and the plants for us so that we will have something to eat. God is present in nature and nothing is left to chance. That is why I like to sit here by the window in order to just observe and to think about things. Going for a walk has become practically impossible because I am having such a hard time getting around any more. Yet, in spite of everything, sitting here I have the opportunity to observe the changes of the seasons. And all the things the good Lord has created." Although this old woman may not have had the education of Dag Hammerskjöld, she, too, was extremely close to what he wrote about, to experiencing the fulfillment of one's life.

Ignatius completed his *Spiritual Exercises* with the "Contemplation to Attain Love." He encourages the retreatant to ask for "interior knowledge of all the great good I have received, in order that, stirred to profound gratitude, I may become able to love and serve the Divine Majesty in all things" (SE 233). Ignatius proposes a meditation to call to mind the gifts of creation and redemption, and also the special gifts we have received. He encourages the retreatant to ponder "how much God our Lord has done for me, and how much he has given me of what he possesses, and consequently how he, the same Lord, desires to give me even his very self, in accordance with his divine design." It seems to me that the old woman by the window is doing exactly what Ignatius proposed. Ultimate meaning or fulfillment is found in the realization that "the Lord desires to give me even his self." We are, indeed, being prepared to accept God's gift of himself and thus to attain complete union with God.

CHAPTER FIVE

AN INNER CENTER OF STILLNESS

The older we get, the more we are confronted with the fact that the opportunities for human interaction decrease simply because we can no longer hear, see, or walk all that well. While these are painful losses, they can also be seen as nature's invitation to search our soul more deeply. If we were to decline this invitation, we would suffer an even greater loss. It goes without saying that the prayer life of an eighty-year-old differs from that of a twenty-five-year-old. It probably is more mature and profound, but it is certainly also rife with its own particular challenges. How are we to pray when we are old? What can help us whenever we wish to pray?

When he was head of the United Nations, Dag Hammerskjöld established a meditation room in its headquarters in New York City to which diplomats, employees, and visitors—regardless of religion—could retreat for meditation and quiet time. He wrote an inspirational text in his own hand and placed it into the room. The first sentence of this text read: "In each of us there is a center of stillness surrounded by silence." By this inner center of stillness, he likely meant what the classic spiritual tradition of the mystics has referred to as the "fine tip of the soul." Hammerskjöld rightfully insisted that this center of stillness exists already in each one of us. We do not need to create it. All we need to do is find the spot where it can be accessed. It may be that the path has been traveled little and is overgrown. Perhaps it still needs to be cleared. But as we get older, Mother Nature makes it a little bit easier for us to follow this path to the center. And yet, we quickly discover that it is not all that easy to maintain our concentration, since this is one of our faculties that is in decline. This is a shortcoming of old age that we must simply accept. Blessed are those who do not feel guilty because of this nature-imposed burden; for that would not be healthy. Modern methods of meditation emphasize that the body must be incorporated in the contemplation. What this advice means here is that we have to accept the infirmities of old age and to hold them up to God. This is not always easy.

Many people fall into the trap of idealizing prayer at this time of life. While still young, some put off prayer until the latter stages of life when they will have more leisure in which to do their praying, only to discover, when they have gotten old, how difficult and disappointing prayer can be at this point. The deeper the roots of prayer are laid early in life, the easier it will be to tap into them and fortify them at an advanced age.

One can pray jointly with other people in a community or in a group, or together with just one other person. Of course, many people will want to pray alone. A church or a chapel is normally the most suitable place for prayer; still, such locations are not always readily accessible, or even suitable. One can pray in one's home, designating a particular prayer space and setting it aside by means of a cross or another type of religious artwork as a focal point.

There are many forms of prayer. The primary form of prayer is the celebration of the eucharist to which Jesus himself invites us, saying, "Do this in memory of me." With these words we touch the very core of the celebration of the eucharist. We remember how Jesus lived, suffered, died, and rose from the dead to ascend into heaven. We also remember how he wants to be among us as the center of our lives. The celebration of the eucharist wants to move Jesus to the center of our attention, affection, and devotion. This memory turns automatically into an expression of gratitude, which is precisely what celebrating the eucharist means; indeed, the Greek original means, "giving thanks." Everything for which we are grateful will then become one great act of gratitude. There is even room for our concerns and petitions. The highlight of this gratitude is reached when Jesus gives himself to us in his body and in his blood. Thus he does exactly that which is characteristic of our God: God wants to give himself to us. This is the very nature of the passion of God which is embodied in Jesus and demonstrated throughout his life. If we are no longer able to go to church or to the chapel where the holy eucharist is celebrated, we can watch the Mass on television as a source of comfort and spiritual strength. A woman taking care of old people once mentioned gratefully to me the joy of elderly people following the celebration of the eucharist this way: "There is peace reflected in their eyes and sometimes a kind of brightness."

The official prayer of the church is the Liturgy of the Hours in which the Psalms play a major part. St. Augustine expressed it as follows: "Christ prays for us as our priest; he prays in us as our head and we pray to him as our God. Let us recognize our voice in him and his voice in us." People who pray in this fashion do so knowing that they are praying in unison with the entire church; for they participate in a prayer that perennially rises up to God from all corners of the earth. They also are praying for all the needs of the world, those that are known and those that are unknown. There are lay people who recite the complete Liturgy of the Hours. Others pray parts of it, especially the morning and the evening prayer. They pray in groups, even as couples, or alone. The Liturgy of the Hours constitutes a rich source of prayer and a very meaningful method of praying each day.

More common is praying the rosary. It is the preferred prayer of many older people. The rosary can be prayed in groups or individually. In some retirement homes, parish churches, and chapels, people gather at a certain time of the day and pray the rosary together. A fellow Jesuit of mine who frequently accompanies students to Albania, the poorest country in Europe, in order to support the reconstruction efforts of the Jesuits there, told me how people assembled in a square under the shade of trees every Sunday. There they would recite the prayers of the rosary in an Oriental-sounding monotone. One could sense how serious and important a practice this was. During the Communist dictatorship, any form of religious activity was suppressed. Praying was punished with imprisonment or even with the kidnapping of family members. My confrere spoke about this to a thirty-four-year-old Albanian named Zef. "These ten fingers"—he was showing him his work-worn hands—"and the recollection of the mysteries of the rosary, the incarnation, the suffering, and the glorification of Jesus have allowed us to remain Christians without the benefit of bibles and sacraments. Only the rosary made it possible for us to cling to our faith."

It was hardly two weeks into his elevation to the papacy when another person, Karol Wojtyla, who had personally witnessed and suffered under a Communist regime, spoke warmly in a sermon at the Sunday Angelus about praying the Angelus, praying the rosary, and how he had incorporated his new service as pope into his daily routine of reciting it. At the beginning of the twenty-fifth year of his pontificate, on October 16, 2002, by then old and frail, he once again recommended the rosary to us in a very personal tone in an apostolic letter. On this occasion he added to the usual mysteries—the joyful, sorrowful, and glorious mysteries—five additional mysteries in conjunction with Jesus' public life, calling them the luminous mysteries:

1. The Baptism in the Jordan
2. The Wedding at Cana
3. The Proclamation of the Kingdom
4. The Transfiguration
5. The Institution of the Eucharist

These new mysteries of the rosary are especially recommended for Thursday prayers.

The petitionary prayer, often in more personalized form and in one's own words, is probably the most natural form of prayer for many people. Parents pray for their children and grandchildren. Nobody has to be taught how to do that. Just as there is no need to teach children to tell their wishes to their parents, every believer is privileged to ask God for favors because he or she is a child of God. That is part of any intimate relationship in which people trust one another.

Since God already knows and does not forget about our needs, we do not pray to inform him about them; we rather place them into his hands, and by entrusting them to him we turn them over to him. Thus petitionary prayers are liberating and beneficial. We no longer have to carry our burden on our own. God knows about us. Sometimes we fail to understand him, but we believe in him, in his presence, in his secret works, and in his goodness. Thus our heart becomes ready to receive his gifts. Every petitionary prayer should conclude with the words: "Not my will but yours be done" (Lk 22:42). That too is part of the relationship of trust. There are people who speak these words too early and too readily because they do not truly trust that God will listen to their prayers and are attempting to protect themselves from disappointment. There are also people who express these words of submission too late or not at all. Then their prayers become fanatical and unhealthy. It is as if they were going to force God into doing something. This, too, is an area where we must discover our own way and find the right balance.

When we petition God in our prayers we are never alone. St. Paul writes about the transfigured Jesus in his letter to the Hebrews that he "always lives to make intercession for them [i.e. those who approach God through him]" (Heb 7:25). A different translation reads "in order to be their advocate." As friends of God, the saints work hand in hand with Jesus. The entire host of saints, whom nobody is able to count, are gathered around Jesus and, together with him, they act in our behalf in great solidarity, presenting our needs to God. Through petitionary prayer we participate now, here on earth, in this activity taking place in heaven. Older people enjoy the privilege of practicing this activity. Many do so spontaneously by professing their faith, voicing their concerns, and through their love. In the Society of Jesus, this is the official task with which the older confreres, who are no longer pursuing an active life, are entrusted. Thus, in the list of names that is published annually by every province for internal use, each elderly confrere gets the following notation added to his name: *orat pro ecclesia et societate,* i.e. he is praying for the church and the Society of Jesus. During my almost nine years at the Berlin retirement home, I noticed with great joy how seriously this task was taken.

Petitionary prayer goes hand in hand with the prayer of thanksgiving. We have already discussed gratitude in the previous chapter. It goes without saying that it is also expressed through prayer. Prayers of thanksgiving and petitionary prayers supplement and stimulate one another.

There are many prayers available to us from the wealth of the Christian tradition. This rich tradition enhances our own prayer life and reveals perspectives that we would not be able to discover on our own. Many people create their own individual prayers in which they express to God their personal experiences, concrete gratitude, and specific concerns. Gradually, this personal prayer develops into a treasured resource that draws us nearer to God in a unique way.

Normally, prayer becomes quieter and quieter. Sometimes it turns into quiet lingering in the loving benevolence of God. It feels good to dwell in his presence. There is no longer any need for a great many words, since God already knows everything. Whatever joys and sufferings, needs and concerns, successes and failures that we consciously remember, we can simply share with God, placing them in his hands. God looks at us lovingly and with immeasurable benevolence. He rejoices in our existence. That suffices. We are forever in his loving gaze.

In a well-known story told about Jean Vianney, the parish priest of the remote French hamlet of Ars, the holy priest noticed a farmer sitting regularly and for long periods of time in a pew of his church. One day, he asked the farmer what he was doing there. The farmer replied: "God is looking at me and I am looking at him." In these simple words, the very core of prayer is concisely and appropriately expressed. Many of us have been able to make a similar discovery on our own, deriving from it a deep and quiet happiness. Without any effort, we hold up to God ourselves as well as all those who are dear to our heart. This is the way it should be.

CHAPTER SIX

DEVOTION

One of the fundamental principles of life is that growth always requires a letting go. Noted psychologists attribute the source of all neurotic disturbances to a refusal to move on, to grow up and become an adult and to surrender everything that is no longer relevant. As people get older, greater emphasis is spontaneously placed on letting go and less emphasis is placed on the new things into which one grows. That is why it is appropriate for the aging person to make an effort to remain receptive to new things and events. As mentioned previously, at the age of seventy-five, the severely ill Pedro Aruppe had the following words from his final message to the Society of Jesus read to the community: "To those who share my age, I urgently recommend openness. We must find out what needs to be done now, and we must do so emphatically."

For the most part, the task of letting go is a painful experience, yet one we must willingly embrace. There is no room for self-deception or procrastination. It is a process we must allow to occur in a spirit of genuine devotion, i.e. dedication and surrender, despite the likely normal feelings of resistance. This process takes place in many areas of life. By this time in our lives, most of us already own fewer material things, are less energetic, and are less capable of resistance. We have fewer responsibilities and are no longer included in as many plans and events. Frequently our mobility becomes more limited, our outside contacts become fewer, and relationships end or fade away. We count more friends among the deceased than the living; some of our certainties and convictions lose their strength: empty rooms are inhabited only by memories. We discover unimagined forms of poverty, and are robbed of our dignity. At times, we may even feel naked. There are many who have found comfort in Jesus' words to Peter: "Very truly, I tell you, when you were younger, you used to fasten your own belt and to go wherever you wished. But when you grow old, you will stretch out your hands, and someone else will fasten a belt around and take you where you do not wish to go" (Jn 21:18). At the same time, there is the danger of authoritarian behavior in those who are helped as well as in those who are offering assistance. Time and again, we must seek a new balance between the poles of acceptance and resistance—a strenuous and sometimes awkward task. But we should remember that "letting go" is, after all, an active verb.

A fellow Jesuit imagines meeting Christ in the following way: In a large, bright, and cheerfully decorated banquet hall there is a long table. Jesus is sitting at the head as host. Assembled around the table are many figures whose identities are unclear, but each one represents a part of himself. Together they comprise his entire being, everything that makes up his personality. Some of the figures are familiar, but most of them are not. Christ invited all of them to this banquet; no one was forgotten or excluded. As he looked at them all, it was shocking. Next, he had to welcome each manifestation of his personality and seat them at their assigned places at the table: his various physical shapes, his memories, his feelings of guilt, his fears. . . . He was shocked when his elderly self enters the hall and speaks to him about what is happening to him. He tells him: "Slowly but surely I will take something away from you. Maybe I will start with your teeth, then your hair, then your smooth face, then your memory. . . . Each time you will have a choice. If you voluntarily surrender what I want I will return it to your Creator as a gift from you. However, if you resist, I will simply take it away from you and carry it into your grave." This imaginary encounter may perhaps serve as a vivid and drastic commentary on Jesus' words: "For those who want to save their life will lose it, and those who lose their life for my sake will find it" (Mt 16:25).

Perhaps the act of letting go must extend considerably beyond our own planning. People who have lived their entire lives based on faith, and who have strengthened the faith of others, occasionally enter a dark night of doubting their own faith and of inner insecurity during the final phases of their lives. This may turn into a rather painful experience during the course of which the aging person is robbed of all self-assurance and forced to engage in blind surrender. During the final months of her brief life, Thérèse of Lisieux (1873–1897) experienced this type of darkness so vividly that she became convinced that she had completely lost her faith. This was an extremely painful form of alienation for a Carmelite nun who had been so uncompromising in the way she had built her entire life on faith. "God is like a wall," she kept saying. Still, even during this Gethsemani-like trial, she remained faithful, managing even frequently to repeat that everything is God's grace. On the other hand, there are people who will be privileged to approach death without any kind of noticeable doubt and to return their soul to the Creator. God's ways are inscrutable, and rightfully so. *"Si comprehendis, non es Deus,"* St. Augustus insisted: "The moment you understand (an event or somebody), it won't be God."

One essential characteristic of God is that he wishes to give of himself. God is both communication and self-revelation to the fullest extent. And that is precisely what continuously takes place in the mystery of the Trinity. The Father gives himself completely to the Son so that the fullness of the Father becomes existentially identical with the Son and the Son with the Father. The Son yields completely to the Father without any reservation or without exercising any restraint. He completely embodies the spirit of devotion, dedication, and surrender. By creating the world, God wishes to give himself completely to humanity. In the life of Jesus, this complete dedication and surrender continues, "for I always do what is pleasing to him" (Jn 8:29). He even sacrifices himself for humanity "to the point of death—even death on the cross" (Phil 2:7). In the celebration of the Eucharist, this self-sacrifice of Jesus is eternalized. God embodies the perennial dynamics of dedication and surrender, i.e. of giving himself.

Thus every human being's most important characteristic is his or her receptivity. The act of letting go that occurs progressively in old age is already a form of preparation and practice for the ultimate act of letting go during the final hour of our existence here on earth. During the hour of death, one must leave everything behind, people as well as material things, and face death all alone. But letting go does not constitute the end; it rather prepares us for the great reception when we experience complete fulfillment in the presence of God: "But, as it is written, 'What no eye has seen, nor ear heard, nor the human heart conceived, what God has prepared for those who love him'" (1 Cor 2:9). Nobody's life will come up empty; it will rather be directed to a kind of fullness we cannot even begin to imagine.

Perhaps the most important tasks during the process of aging are dedication and surrender. Jesus' final words before his death in the Gospel according to Luke are words of this kind of devotion: "Father, into your hands I commend my spirit'" (Lk 23:46, which is a quote from Ps 31:6). It forms a compact prayer of dedication and surrender, and it is good practice to prayerfully repeat these words together with Jesus. These words can accompany our bright as well as our dark hours: whatever oppresses us or makes us uneasy, whatever makes us feel happy or grateful, whatever comes into consciousness during our conversations or in our recollections, whatever our experiences of impermanence are, there is nothing better for us to do than to hold them up to God and to entrust them to him. We concretely do that by imitating these words of Christ. When we think of specific tragedies—an incurable disease, the loss of a loved one or of a close confidante, the uncertain ending of an important event—in all these cases, devotion is our best and most fruitful position. This does not imply that we need not assume any initiative of our own, but that the initiative we do take will be fine-tuned with God and taken together with him. "If we live, we live to the Lord, and if we die, we die to the Lord; so then, whether we live or whether we die, we are the Lord's" (Rom 14:8).

There are numerous prayers of devotion that are longer than Jesus' entreaty on the cross. They are able to help better articulate and comprehend what is important. Among the Psalms, Psalms 23 and 139 can be particularly helpful. A prayer by the Swiss mystic, Nicholas of Flüe (1417–1482), expresses in highly poetic form an extraordinary longing for and trust in God:

> *My Lord and my God,*
> *take everything from me*
> *that keeps me from Thee.*
> *My Lord and my God,*
> *give everything to me*
> *that brings me near to Thee.*
> *My Lord and my God,*
> *take me away from myself*
> *and give me completely to Thee.*

The prayers of dedication and surrender written by Charles de Foucauld and Ignatius of Loyola are equally beautiful and enriching. The blessed Carmelite Edith Stein of Cologne, the Jesuit Rupert Mayer of Munich, and the martyrs of Lübeck (three young Catholic priests and one Lutheran pastor who were beheaded in 1943), who were all victims of Nazi violence, had their own prayers of dedication and surrender that were anything but noncommittal.

Dedication and surrender are both processes. They must undergo growth and be prayerfully addressed time and again. They are far from being passive; rather, they are the highest form of prayer and its crowning activity. Yet, it is true that God creates them in us. They are not static, not something that one *possesses*; on the contrary, they must be continuously practiced and at the same time be received from God. Nowhere is the cooperation between God and humanity more intimate than here. Dedication and surrender that are merely the fruits of our own endeavor are not complete abandonment, precisely because we are still in control in doing it by ourselves. Complete devotion requires a subtle balance between divine and human effectiveness that is possible only in the very practice of it, just as the balancing required while riding a bicycle can be achieved only while riding it; it will never occur while standing still.

Devotion requires that we receive and accept our lives out of God's hand. Because we trust the hand that has presented us with the gift of existence, we are also able to return it to this very hand. The more we feel safe in God's hand, the easier it will be to let go. No longer will we then cling desperately to all the material things we acquired. Jesus tells the parable of a treasure somebody had discovered in a field, "then in his joy he goes and sells all that he has and buys that field" (Mt 13:44). Such is the kingdom of heaven. During the presentation of Jesus in the Temple, Simeon offers us a beautiful illustration of what dedication and surrender will lead to (Lk 2:25–35). He had recognized in the child, Jesus, the long awaited

Messiah. His eyes saw salvation in this child. Now he will be able to end his life in peace and return it to God. I myself am deeply moved by Rembrandt's painting of this scene (*Simeon with the Christ Child in the Temple,* 1666–69). I am equally moved by the fact that it is Rembrandt's last painting, which he had not completed by the time of his death. Thus, after all the highs and lows of his career, he returned his life to God.

CHAPTER SEVEN

SIMPLICITY AND CLARITY

The primary goal of the *Spiritual Exercises* according to Ignatius is "to order one's life" (SE 21). As we get on in years, taking a systematic look back at our lives is a worthwhile task. Though the years are many, they passed rapidly. Our energies are weakening, as is our sense of duty, our ability and—hopefully too—the drive to achieve external successes. Thus the inward path opens up more than during previous phases of our lives. Much that is superfluous falls away. Sometimes this process is imposed on us by a move to smaller living accommodations. Anyone who has not yet made out a will must now face this delicate task that always necessitates a underlying awareness of our mortality. At the same time, there is also a desire to make a clean sweep of our inner lives. Thus an urge for simplicity begins to grow within us with a promise of both beauty and harmony. Ernest Hemingway once reported how he made a habit of repeatedly going over the first draft of a manuscript in a focused effort to cross out and eliminate words and phrases. The result was a powerful and dense prose, for example, "The Old Man and the Sea" for which he received the Nobel Prize in Literature.

This strong desire to get a perspective of the totality of our life often appears spontaneously. It goes without saying that each of us will experience it in our own special way. Pursuing this aim and allowing the synthesis of our life to unfold is a liberating and life-promoting experience. It leads us once again to question the meaning of life, now perhaps with even greater urgency. People often try to uncover the thread running through their lives and try to integrate the past in the present. Once again, Carl Jung's statement in his *Psychological Reflections* merits our attention: "We cannot change anything unless we accept it." Disappointments and traumatic experiences rise to the surface, demanding that proper attention be given to them, so that even they will be able to bear fruit. Nothing is lost in the presence of God; everything can be turned into something good (cf. Rom 8:28). Through calm and deliberate contemplation, many things that once appeared to be entirely negative experiences are now revealed to be hidden gifts, "blessings in disguise." A passage from the prophet Isaiah can guide us while contemplating our lives in this fashion: "But now thus says the Lord, he who created you, O Jacob, he who formed you, O Israel: Do not fear, for I have redeemed you; I have called you by name, you are mine" (Is 43:1). One can examine one's life from this point of view, perhaps even writing down the story and sharing it with a loved one or close friend. We often need to tell another about the story of our life in a relaxed setting and it will truly be a blessing if the opportunity for doing so should arise.

Now, I would like to discuss two aspects in greater detail, namely the forgiveness we owe others and the forgiveness we need ourselves.

ON OFFERING FORGIVENESS

Throughout his life and teachings, Jesus frequently emphasized that we must forgive one another. Even in his answer to the disciples request for a method of prayer, he included the need for forgiveness in a provocative and interesting way: "And forgive us our debts, as we also have forgiven our debtors" (Mt 6:12). He himself had forgiven others their debts and sins. Shortly before his death he prayed, "Father, forgive them; for they do not know what they are doing" (Lk 23:34). It is significant that in this instance he did not forgive on his own authority as he did elsewhere, but rather asked the Father: His heroic example reinforces his teachings for us.

Forgiveness can be rather difficult. At this point in our lives we can appreciate and respect the effort it takes to grant forgiveness. Attempting to force another person to forgive somebody is, in itself, a contradiction and anything but helpful. Let us allow others and ourselves the necessary time to become mature enough to forgive. It is impossible to force the act of forgiveness. Those who attempt to take this step in a hasty and inauthentic way will soon notice how weak is the ground on which they are standing. This ought not be taken as an excuse for putting forgiveness off, but rather for taking forgiveness seriously.

There is a dire need for forgiveness. Aggression and violence are on the increase in our world. One can see it simply by watching television, driving a car, attending a sports event, or visiting a school. The river of violence can only be diverted through forgiveness. Pope John Paul II never tires of emphasizing that there will be no peace without justice and no justice without forgiveness. In 1960, at Easter, Dag Hammerskjöld wrote into his diary: "Forgiveness breaks the chain of causes." Without forgiveness we will remain prisoners of the vicious circle between violence and injustice.

There are several common misunderstandings which should be addressed. First is the misconception that forgiveness is some kind of foolish naiveté that polishes over every wrong and interprets evil away so that there is nothing left to forgive any more. One cannot escape this difficult task so easily. Forgiveness is much more serious than that.

Nor is forgiveness a form of suppression that seeks peace at any price, avoiding a confrontation with injustice. Suppression can never serve as a lasting solution to a problem. To vent one's anger may cause conflict and hostility, but swallowing and suppressing one's anger has a price tag too. It can lead to fatigue and depression. Anger is a poison, both in its uncontrolled expression and in its suppression. Forgiveness faces evil squarely and deals with it courageously and wisely.

Forgiveness is not tantamount to forgetting. Any great injustice that we have suffered remains stored in our memory, in our psyche, and sometimes even in our bodies. The injury leaves scars that remind us of what has been done to us. By forgiving we do not forget, but we do remember differently. We remember in a manner that no longer harbors either resentment or bitterness and which no longer chains us to those who have done evil to us. Forgiveness opens a path to the future, while resentment holds us captive in the bad past.

Forgiveness is not a kind of weakness that does not dare to face reality, without conviction and without genuine engagement. On the contrary, forgiveness is courageous and demands strength.

Nor does forgiveness confer impunity. Even if the perpetrator has already been punished by the law or in some other just fashion, the victim will have to forgive. The law deals with "the outside." While it punishes the offender, it does not free the victim. Forgiveness takes place in our very own hearts. On the other hand, forgiving another person his or her malice does not necessarily mean forgoing just punishment under the law.

Courses about the "Art and Science of Forgiveness" commonly define forgiveness as "abandoning the resentment one is entitled to," and therefore abandoning also the desire for revenge and retribution. Thus an effort is made to differentiate between forgiveness and reconciliation. Reconciliation requires at least two persons, while forgiveness can be achieved independently of any contact with the perpetrator. There can be cases in which forgiveness without any attempt at reconciliation is to be preferable, for instance in the case of rape.

Forgiveness is difficult to accomplish because something in our nature wants to keep holding on to our injury. Our justifiable resentment is like a precious, albeit dark, possession. We can withdraw into our injured state, settle down and wallow in it, nurturing our resentment and our pain. Thus it can easily become an obsession. When we hold onto resentment something will eventually die in us—our sense of humor, our spontaneity, our energy, our dreams, or our sense of self-worth. Resentment will also affect our health. Genuine forgiveness relieves us this sinister and destructive baggage. It disarms us of a weapon that we might otherwise keep using against fellow human beings.

Forgiveness is tantamount to becoming more mature: starting out as passive victims without any control over our feelings, we end up acknowledging that we ourselves are the source of our emotions. Forgiveness is the slowly growing insight that we have no control of other people. Thus genuine forgiveness is a great challenge, almost like jumping over one's own shadow. If we fail, we will fall short of completing the development of our personality, of our life in accordance with the truth of the gospel. Even our prayer life will be affected. If we fail to meet this challenge, we will get caught up in a circle of never-ending repetitions that will occasionally turn neurotic. We will have to carry with us the oppressive and suffocating burden of failures, frustrations, foiled plans, and violations of our honor and our feelings. It is not until we forgive that something truly new will enter our world. Then a realm will be created where life will be able to develop freely.

Resisting forgiveness saps our strength; it wastes a lot of vital energy and joy. The ability to forgive is both a blessing and a form of salvation. Normally, forgiveness tends to be a long, drawn-out process. First, we must arrive at the conscious decision of willingly entering into this process. Then, we need a lot of patience to proceed on the road to forgiveness. I like to compare this road to a kind of spiral. Following the spiral pattern, we can indeed make progress, but only by moving in progressive circles that force us to keep going, passing the crucial issue in each round. With each round we must confront the offender, and we must keep forgiving him or her anew each time.

Let us never forget that this entire process occurs through grace. Perhaps, this is why the best place for accomplishing the act of forgiveness is sitting under accompanied by crucifix, looking at Jesus and listening to him and continually repeating with him these words: "Father, forgive them."

ON RECEIVING FORGIVENESS

Our God is a God of forgiveness. The prophet Micah marvels at the joy God derives from forgiving: "Who is a God like you, pardoning iniquity and passing over the transgression" (Mi 7:18–20). And the prophet Zephaniah assures us: "The Lord has taken away the judgments against you . . . he will renew you in his love . . . he will rejoice over you in gladness." (Zep 3:15–17). Martin Buber translates this verse as: "God has revoked his judgment against you . . . God recreates you simply out of his love for you . . . He delights in you." Jesus expresses it much more clearly and convincingly. When the Pharisees and the Scribes get upset over the fact that he is spending time with publicans and sinners, Jesus tells three parables: the Parable of the Lost Sheep, the Parable of the Lost Coin, and the Parable of the Prodigal Son (Lk 15). Each of the three parables has basically the same message; they all highlight the joy of the person finding something or someone. Thus Jesus describes a characteristic image of his father. Prior to that, he had insisted that "no one knows who the Son is except the Father, or who the

Father is except the Son and anyone to whom the Son chooses to reveal him" (Lk 10:22). This is precisely what he wishes to do now: to reveal the Father to us. With this in mind, he describes vividly and emphatically the joy the Father derives from the act of forgiveness. So if we find it difficult to forgive, we are likely to misunderstand the very essence of God, for he loves to forgive us beyond all measure.

Through his short story *The Spanish Rose Tree*, the twentieth-century German writer Werner Bergengrün helped me to better understand the significance of the three parables in Luke's fifteenth chapter. The passage in question reads: "To be sure, love is tested by the its faithfulness, yet it finds fulfillment through forgiveness." God is love. Because love is fulfilled by forgiveness, we can say that God is at his most divine when he forgives. God's joy in the act of forgiveness is very striking, particularly since it illuminates the very depths of God's being. God has many names. In scripture, the use of the Hebrew name of God "Yahweh" is often followed by the phrase "the faithful one," or "the merciful one." These names remind us that God remains faithful to us in spite of our sins, he loves to be merciful, and he is always in a forgiving mood.

There is probably no person alive whose story does not include several episodes of which he or she is particularly ashamed, dreading to remember them or being reminded of them. Except for Jesus and his mother, no human being is completely without sin. Frequently this guilt weighs heavily on people. Today, our understanding of guilt is often quite different from

SUMMONED AT EVERY AGE

its definition throughout most of the last century. A
new sense of social justice and an awareness and
consciousness of guilt has evolved, based less on the
law and more on truthfulness and justice, on dealing
responsibly with the environment. In this new
consciousness, many people judge themselves harshly
because they do not live in accordance with the
demands of justice. However, the psalmist's prayer is
as valid now as it was during biblical times: "To you all
flesh shall come. When deeds of iniquity overwhelm
us, you forgive our transgressions" (Ps 65:3f). Every
human being is in need of forgiveness. The good news,
however, is that Jesus has opened for us the pathway
to our merciful Father.

Jesus stated explicitly that he had come "to call not
the righteous but sinners" (Mt 9:13). That is too bad for
those who are righteous. The angel explains Jesus'
name to Joseph in the following way: "He will save his
people from their sins" (Mt 1:21). His name articulates
his identity. When John the Baptist introduces Jesus,
he refers to him as the Lamb of God: "'Here is the
Lamb of God who takes away the sin of the world'" (Jn
1:29). We are told in so many different ways that
nobody who feels guilty needs to be afraid of Jesus; on
the contrary, it was precisely for these people that he
came. In his compassion he forgives their sins without
humiliating them. He says to the adulteress, "'Woman,
where are they? Has no one condemned you? . . .
Neither do I condemn you. Go your way, and from
now on do not sin again" (Jn 8:10f). It is never too late.
So, during the final hour prior to his death, he tells the
criminal who had just rebuked the other one for

deriding Jesus: "Truly I tell you, today you will be with me in Paradise" (Lk 23:43). Clearly, with Jesus there is salvation in abundance.

Forgiveness cannot be accomplished on our own. It must be given to us. This is a tall order in some people's eyes, particularly those who wish to do everything on their own and by themselves. Yet there is nothing to *do* here, only to receive abundantly. God forgives us in many different ways. The highest form of forgiveness is the sacrament of reconciliation, the gift of Easter instituted and presented by the risen Lord to his church (Jn 20:22f). Above, we emphasized that forgiving others would be an extended process. The same applies to receiving forgiveness. It takes a long time until this miracle is completely internalized and until it reaches the "fine tip of the soul." During the past couple of centuries, the Catholic tradition mostly neglected the work to be done following confession, while preparation was perhaps emphasized too much. There happened to be a tendency to put the confession quickly *behind* us; however, the time following confession is also a process, and this process is not really complete until we have also forgiven ourselves, that is to say, the moment when God's forgiveness has unfolded completely and entirely embraced us.

By receiving God's forgiveness we experience a twofold joy. First, there is the joy of relief. This is entirely natural and healthy. However, this joy is followed by a supernatural joy, that is to say, a sharing in the pleasure God feels when he forgives us. Traces of this divine pleasure inundate us, similar to the way in which the Prodigal Son felt his father's joy when the latter welcomed him back, embracing him lovingly and joyfully. This joy is like balm for the soul of anybody who has ever suffered from guilt. God gladly extends his joy to us.

Giving and receiving forgiveness reflect important tasks for people who have reached a certain age. This is likely our most important contribution to the clarity we need in order to peacefully and confidently complete the final stretches of our lives. There is probably no better way to prepare ourselves for the great journey ahead, awaiting us at the end of our days. Then the Lord will grant us the kind of peace that the world will never be able to grant us nor take from us.

CHAPTER EIGHT

DEATH: A PART OF OUR LIVES

Our culture takes a one-sided view of death, inter-preting it mostly as a kind of defeat. Obituaries are rife with causes of death, listing them as "heart fail-ure" or "circulatory collapse." No doubt, they are accu-rate, but the references to "failure" or "collapse" reveal much about our contemporary image of death. Our age has made enormous technical strides, especially in medicine, but it has a difficult time with the things that are still beyond its control. During my years at the Jesuit retirement facility, I witnessed the death of many fellow Jesuits. The cemetery had always a long waiting list: often burials had to be postponed for ten days after somebody's death—a fact I never quite managed to understand. Nevertheless, the body was picked up by the funeral home within one or two hours of the person's death. There was hardly enough time to say good-bye. I always thought that this was symptomatic of a culture that seeks to hide the reality of death. Something is missing in such a culture. People do not sufficiently respect that dying is not merely a failure, but also the ultimate completion of a person's life.

Etty Hillesum, as a young Jewish woman, witnessed the German occupation of Amsterdam and the persecution of Jews there during the Second World War. On July 3, 1942, at the age of 28, she wrote in her diary:

> I was looking our (i.e. the Jews') destruction in the eye, our presumably miserable end that is manifest-ing itself already in the many ordinary moments of daily life. It was this possibility that I incorporated into the perception of my life without subsequently

experiencing a lessening of my vitality. . . . The possibility of death is an absolute presence in my life, and, because of it, my life has acquired an additional dimension: I now look death and destruction in the eye, accepting them as a part of life. It would be a big mistake to sacrifice a part of one's life to death by fearing the latter and by trying to fight it off. Both resistance and fear leave us with a miserably atrophied remnant of life one can hardly call life at all. It sounds almost paradoxical: If we marginalize death in our lives, life will never be complete. On the contrary, by incorporating death into our lives we expand and enrich our lives. I have no personal experience with regard to death. I haven't been touched by it." I have never seriously considered death's reality. I have never had any time for thinking about it. And now, death has come into my life for the first time, with all its might; yet death has appeared like an old acquaintance who is a part of my life and who must be accepted. This is all rather simple. There is no need for profound reflection. Death entered my life unexpectedly, mighty and simple and matter-of-factly, and almost without causing a stir. Death has taken up residence in my life, and I now realize that death is a part of life.

Every individual's death is unique. Often, although not always, people die the way they lived. In this respect, the death of a person confirms that dying is a part of living. A very old Jesuit confided to a confrere that he was no longer able to see any meaning or purpose in his life. However, the truth was that he was only waiting for God, "as a deer longs for flowing streams" (Ps 42), curious to find out about the appearance of God to whom he had dedicated his life and whom he would soon encounter face-to-face. He prayed that he would die in his sleep during the night, yet always added humbly that not his, but God's will be done. Life offers us many opportunities to practice dying. Thus death will not ultimately come as a surprise. Together with one of the criminals crucified with Jesus we can pray: "Remember me when you come into your kingdom" (Lk 23:42).

When we celebrate the eucharist, we pray together "until you return in glory." We can interpret these words personally and apply them to the coming of Christ during the hour of our death; for there is only *one* coming of the Lord—continuously—that will be completed in the future. This reflects God's yearning for us more than our yearning for him. "I am my beloved's and his desire is for me," says the bride in the *Song of Songs* (Sg 7:10). These words apply to every one of us; they make our lives, especially our final hour, meaningful. "His desire is for me."

Through the prophet Hosea, God speaks to the people of Israel as if to a bride, that he will "allure her . . . and speak tenderly to her" (Hos 2:16). According to the New Testament, we may interpret these words as applying to ourselves. It is indeed a charming image that expresses an even more gladsome reality. Our God is determined to get our attention and to win our affection and devotion. The deeper meaning of our lives lies in the realization that God's love seeks *us* with such enormous intensity. Here lie also the roots of our existence: God's yearning for us. Mother Theresa, Thérèse of Lisieux, and the great Teresa of Avila together understood the words of the crucified Jesus, "I am thirsty" (Jn 19:28) in this sense. Jesus is thirsty for our love. In these words, these three great women saw a powerful motivation to do their utmost for Jesus and to devote their lives to him, each one in her own inimitable way. They met the God of love who liberates us from fear. He is the God who does not want *anything* from us, but who seeks us completely and passionately.

Of course, it stands to reason that our image of God plays a significant role during our life's journey toward death. A lot depends on how we picture God. Those who see God primarily in the role of a severe judge who is rigorously judging our lives from birth to death will have a difficult time looking forward to death. Sad to say, many Christians view God in this role, especially since there are passages in scripture that promote this very image. Yet the main message of the Bible does not portray God in this light. The image of the Father that Jesus mediated to us is not harsh. Rather, God is the faithful one. "I have loved you with an everlasting love; therefore I have continued my faithfulness to you" (Jer 31:3). Thus in saying, "God is love" (1 Jn 4:8; 16), John succinctly portrays God. This love is everlasting. A God who would love us merely for as long as we live, would be nothing but a caricature. Jesus berates the Sadducees who share this view, telling them, "you are quite wrong" (Mk 12:27). We would be completely wrong if we were to think of God in those terms. His love extends beyond death and lasts for all eternity. The joy we experience when we meet God is identical with our eternal bliss.

However, there is another consideration: When we encounter this great love, we will see our own lives with great clarity, in the light of his love. When we encounter God face-to-face we will be painfully glimpsing the many missed opportunities during our journey on earth. God won't have to tell us a thing because what we see will speak for itself. This is perhaps what we traditionally refer to as purgatory. However, let me repeat that throughout the entire encounter God remains at the center as the one who loves abundantly and infinitely. It is this very center that provides both a place and a direction for everything else.

The fact that death is a part of life has practical consequences, too. During the most recent general congregation, the Jesuits set a new goal for themselves living in this contemporary society, one that could never have been considered in the days of the founder. Today, part of our faithful responsibility can be expressed in the way that it is expressed in the Complimentary Norms to the Constitutions of the Society of Jesus:

> In view of today's medical advances—on the one hand, the possibility of extending human life beyond its natural duration, and, on the other hand, aiding others through the donation of human organs—and inspired by our faith in Jesus Christ, everyone should leave advance instructions in accordance with prevailing law about the moment of transition from earthly to eternal life, reflect ways of better expressing our personal dignity and our solidarity with other human beings.

The noted Jesuit theologian Karl Rahner once gave me a memorial card of his mother who had died on July 27, 1976, at the age of 101. On the front was a picture of a spry old lady with friendly, clear eyes. On the back, there was printed a prayer by Pierre Teilhard de Chardin that she had carried with her throughout the final years of her life. The Rahner children had the printer add the following inscription below the poem: "Prayer for a peaceful death; handwritten by our mother." It seems a fitting conclusion to this chapter.

> Now that I have recognized you as the one who is my extended self, let me recognize you in my final hour in the shape of every alien and hostile power that wishes to destroy me, or to thrust me aside when my body or my mind show the signs of wear caused by old age. When the evil that diminishes us attacks me externally or rises up internally; during the painful moment when I suddenly realize that I am sick and that I am getting old; especially during that final moment when I feel that I am about to leave my physical self behind; during all these sinister hours, please, Lord, let me understand that it is you who, providing that my faith will be strong enough, will take great pains to push aside the fibers of my existence in order to get to the very marrow of my being and to pull me inside of you.
>
> —PIERRE TEILHARD DE CHARDIN

CHAPTER NINE

LONELINESS

For many elderly people, loneliness is a painful experience. It is difficult to cope with, especially if one's spouse has passed away, or if one of them had to be admitted into a nursing home. "Nobody needs me," one assumes. "Hardly anybody visits me. They've all forgotten about me, they don't have any time." There comes a point where being alone can't be downplayed any more. The feeling of isolation becomes a daily burden. At this point in our lives, Jesus' frequent and compassionate words about the poor and the little children can be applied to us.

Without wanting in any way to minimize the suffering and loneliness we often experience, I would like to add that being alone is not a negative experience in itself. Someone who is able to fill those hours of solitude will be able to turn them into a blessing. However, someone who is not successful in this will find that being alone is a source of suffering. That is why it would be wrong to battle solitude at any cost. It is likewise a mistake to constantly complain about it. Above all, we must face loneliness and face it squarely. Although it can be hard and painful, being alone can be fruitful, even a blessing, but only if we accept it. It can be an invitation to look beyond any limitations and set out to look for treasures yet unknown. The experience of loneliness may reveal an inner emptiness that will turn destructive if we reject or deny it, yet it can just as well lead us to great depths where we will enter a grace-filled union with God. Every Christian is a temple of the Holy Spirit and a dwelling place of the triune God. No human being can bestow final fulfillment on us. There will always be remnants of emptiness and distance that will remain unbridgeable. That is a fact of human existence. Only those who accept it will find peace. Those who reject it will remain forever dissatisfied. Sometimes, the problem is not the fact of being alone but the inability to change solitude into a meaningful experience.

Among the belongings of a confrere who had died, the superior found the following quotation by the poet and graphic artist Gotthard de Beauclair (1907–1992)— unfortunately with no specific reference to the context in which he had written it:

> After the noon hour, the light becomes precious.
> In the shadows, the birth of the stars commences.
> The great silence.
> You are alone, but not lonesome.

Talking about this subject in general terms is rather delicate. There is a danger that those who suffer from loneliness will get the impression that they must not complain but simply accept the pain. There is no doubt that there is a kind of loneliness that can turn destructive and cannot be overcome simply by willpower. In other words, there is most certainly a kind of loneliness that requires help and human contact in order to safeguard against falling any deeper and losing all one's vitality. It is quite possible that, with the help of others, we will be able to identify the kind of solitude and isolation that affects us negatively.

Initially, we can try to take advantage of solitude, channeling it as positively as possible. Thus we can discover to some extent how our individual personalities can adapt to the new experience of loneliness and find some positive element in it. At the same time, we must be prepared to determine realistically the amount of interaction with others that we require, and make every effort to maintain and cultivate or to establish it. If at all possible,· it is advisable to take an active approach rather than waiting passively for someone else to reach out.

It certainly would prove to be a wrong strategy if we looked for a solution to our struggles with solitude by seeking solace in alcohol or prescription drugs. That only leads to a dead end. It is also harmful to plunge into excessive activity, making it impossible to find time to even think of loneliness. Old age should be a time without any stress.

Just as we have done throughout our lives, the highest goal at this stage should be to love and trust more. All love and trust are ultimately directed toward God. But God becomes visible to us in our fellow human beings. Even in old age there are new opportunities to discover ways to make this possible. The best way to overcome one's loneliness is to seek contact—to the degree that this is reasonably possible—with other lonely people. This is a splendid way in which to fill loneliness with love. Perhaps it will be possible to get a group of people together who will meet periodically and keep in touch in other ways as well. In some parishes, volunteers regularly visit people who are living alone and who experience loneliness. The result can be the blossoming of mutually beneficial relationships.

Those who support older people, helping them regardless of their needs, are naturally first in line to receive their gratitude and love in a genuine and spontaneous form, just as they, in turn, are offering their services without any ulterior motives and with suitable respect. I am discussing this reciprocal relationship at the end of this book in order to be able to add a few comments about the environment and social condition of aging people. It appears to me that the principal requirement for the services rendered by those who assist older people is the need for accepting the fact that they, too, will get older some day, even if those days are currently just a distant thought. Anyone who denies his or her future loss of vitality will in some way transfer this attitude to people of advanced age. By interacting and maintaining contact with older people we confront our own future aging process. On closer inspection, many a problem occurring among the aged is a question that really concerns all human beings. Ignatius had a firm belief in the dignity of every human being. According to him, great respect for every individual person was the logical consequence of the dignity of each human being. In his *Spiritual Diary*, he frequently reports that he had been praying for "humility, respect, and reverence." These habits, he writes, are not supposed to be "inspired by fear but by love, and have become so deeply embedded into my consciousness that I kept repeating: 'Give me loving humility.' And I prayed equally for respect and reverence." This humble respect is directed primarily to God in the form of veneration, but also to all human beings because Ignatius sensed that God was dwelling in them. According to Ignatius, this was one of the many ways through which he "discovered God in everything." This presence of God in everything characterized his entire life and above all also his encounter with fellow human beings. Loving and humble respect is due in a very special way to all elderly and frail people.

After the death of her brother from cancer following an extended illness at the age of fifty-three, one woman wrote the following in a letter she sent to me: "Although the death of my brother had appeared completely incomprehensible to us, nevertheless, we have come to realize that the experience of accompanying somebody in sickness and in death is a deeply moving and profound privilege that can change one's life." Many people have had a similar experience. It is not possible to explain the reason for this mystery, yet it moves us profoundly and significantly affects our own lives.

In recent decades, the Hospice Movement has developed novel forms of taking care of the most seriously ill, concentrating on the respect for the dignity of the sick and their needs. The concept of hospice constitutes "a combination of medical and nursing care that no longer attempts to extend human life and the process of dying by means of excessive use of modern technology in the futile attempt of curing the terminally ill." Instead, hospice provides palliative care, that is, relief for patients by means of medical and human care in accordance with the realistic needs of terminally ill people. During the course of discussions about death and human companionship at this stage in life, psychological and pastoral help, as well as the care provided by relatives, can be more important than additional chemotherapy or a nearly hopeless surgery. Hospice care can be provided in a facility in a separate wing of a hospital, in the form of home care with the support of caring relatives, or in a combination of all of these efforts. The insights gathered from studies about hospice care confirm that, for instance, the fear of dying or the internal torment of still unsolved human conflicts, etc., frequently turn out to be a greater burden and are more painful than the actual physical pain. The quality of life is not determined primarily by the availability and administration of medical help but more so by the contributions of family, relatives, and social and religious influences.

A Dutch physician once told me about an elderly, childless couple where the husband had become severely ill. Based on the medical evidence, the physician soon established that there was no longer any real chance of recovery. She cautiously, carefully, and calmly informed the patient of the inevitable, while simultaneously promising to do everything in her power to limit and alleviate his pain. During the weeks that followed, both the husband and the wife kept noticing that they were frequently arguing with one another, even though they did not want that and despite the fact that they had never before argued to such an extent. During regular visits to her patient's home, the doctor witnessed this uncharacteristic tension between them. She began to wonder, trying to figure out what she could do about it. The couple was not religious; the doctor, however, was Catholic and lived her life fully conscious of her faith. She therefore made a habit of praying for her seriously ill patients, commending them to God and even keeping a tall, old Easter candle burning in her home in front of a statue of the Virgin Mary. During her next visit, she purposely told the patient and his wife about her prayers in order to signal to the couple that she did not restrict herself merely to her medical tasks, but that she had also included them in her concerns and prayers. Learning about the doctor's concerns changed the way the two people then treated one another and brought them peace and tranquility. They felt surrounded and supported by the doctor's respect and faith, drawing from them the strength to continue despite the loss of so many sureties that had until then provided them with ways of steadying and anchoring their lives.

In the case of Catholic patients, communion for the sick, brought with reverence and devotion, can be genuinely comforting. If at all possible, the rite for "Communion of the Sick" is recommended. It begins with a brief, relaxed conversation in conjunction with a greeting, followed by the introduction of the liturgy (veneration of the holy eucharist, a song, introductory prayer, confession of sins, and a request for forgiveness), a prayer service (for instance by reading the gospel from the previous Sunday, followed by a brief interpretation and prayers for the people), the reception of communion (The Lord's Prayer, invitation to take communion, reception of communion), a song from the hymnal read out loud and the conclusion (prayer with a blessing and a song or prayer to Mary).

In its entirety, the ritual may last for half an hour, but it will be time well spent. This rite offers many possibilities for fruitful volunteer services by extraordinary ministers of the eucharist. Of course, it will be important to refrain from forcing the communion for the sick on anybody, but rather offering it freely.

As we have seen throughout this short book, aging is a process. There are many factors that contribute to our physical, emotional, and spiritual well being during this time of life. The environment that encompasses all areas of life plays an important role— the support and care of loved ones, the affection and cordiality of friends, the physical therapy and creative activities in which we participate, and of course the spiritual support we receive from others. In emphasizing that spirituality is an integral part of the aging process, I am speaking also to those who accompany older people on their journey. God entrusted us to one another, and during the final phases of our lives this alliance will be particularly necessary. In the words of St. Paul: we all form one body, and God assembled the body in such a way that all its members respect and take care of one another (1 Cor 12:24). In this manner, God wishes to lead everything to good—even through us.

A P P E N D I X

MEDITATIONS AND PRAYERS

Remain Young

Nobody gets old simply because he or she has been getting on in years. People get old as soon as they wave their ideals good-bye. As we get older, our skin gets wrinkly; however, if we stop being enthusiastic, our soul will get wrinkly too. Worries, doubts, a lack of self-confidence, fear, and hopelessness, all of these are present throughout the long, long years, forcing the head down to the ground and bending the upright spirit until it touches the dust.

You are as young as your confident optimism, as old as your doubts, as young as your hopes, as old as your dejection. As long as the message of the beauty, the joy, the boldness, the greatness, and the might of the earth, and of humanity and the infinite realm are touching your heart, you will remain young. You will have truly begun to age when your wings are beginning to point downward and the core of your heart will be covered by the snow of pessimism and the ice of cynicism.

—ALBERT SCHWEITZER

I Am Growing Older

Lord, Thou knowest better than I know myself, that I am growing older and will some day be old. Keep me from the fatal habit of thinking I must say something on every subject and every occasion. Release me from craving to straighten out everybody's affairs.

Make me thoughtful, but not moody; helpful, but not bossy. With my vast store of wisdom, it seems a pity not to use it all, but Thou knowest Lord that I want a few friends at the end.

Keep my mind free from the recital of endless details; give me wings to get to the point. Seal my lips from aches and pains. They are increasing, and love of rehearsing them is becoming sweeter as the years go by. I dare not ask for grace enough to enjoy the tales of others' pains, but help me to endure them with patience.

I dare not ask for improved memory, but for a growing humility and a sureness when my memory seems to clash with the memories of others. Teach me the glorious lesson that occasionally I may be mistaken.

Keep me reasonably sweet. I know that I am not a saint—some of them are so hard to live with—but a sour old person is one of the crowning works of the devil.

Give me the ability to see good things in unexpected places, and talents in unexpected people. And give me, O Lord, the grace to tell them so. Amen.

—A SEVENTEENTH CENTURY ENGLISH NUN

Beatitudes for the Aging

Blessed are those who have the courage to do nothing.
They demonstrate to us a different level of living for
one another.

Blessed are those who no longer expect anything and
yet are able to smile.
God's goodness is shining through them.

Blessed are those who are able to listen without
harping on the same issue.
They make our inflexible views more relative.

Blessed are those who endure their powerlessness
without rebelling against it.
They calm our agitated hearts.

Blessed are those who do not dwell in bitterness of
living alone.
They put time in God's hands.

Blessed are those who never tire of showing
confidence.
They are giving us the courage to face every day with
renewed enthusiasm.

Blessed are those who can no longer help others, but
who weep for us.
Their tears will carry a lot of weight in the eyes of God.

Blessed are those who pass their days peacefully and
quietly.
They are creating safe havens for us.

Blessed are those who have nothing to say any longer,
yet do not fall silent.
Their words announce hope and confident optimism.

Blessed are those who empty their hands and extend
their arms.
They are teaching us to cling to nothing.

Blessed are those who do not consider their own
needs all that important and instead only look out
for others.

What would our life be without them?

—BEATRIX KOLK, O.S.B.

Desiderata

Go placidly amid the noise and haste,
and remember what peace there may be in silence.

As far as possible without surrender
be on good terms with all persons.

Speak your truth quietly and clearly
and listen to others,
even the dull and ignorant;
they too have their story.

Avoid loud and aggressive persons,
they are vexations to the spirit.

If you compare yourself with others,
you may become vain and bitter,
for always there will be greater
and lesser persons than yourself.

Enjoy your achievements as well as your plans.

Keep interested in your own career, however humble;
it is a real possession in the changing future of time.
Exercise caution in your business affairs,
for the world is full of trickery.
But let this not blind you to what virtue there is;
many persons strive for high ideals
and everywhere life is full of heroism.

Be yourself.

Especially, do not feign affection.
Neither be cynical about love,
for in the face of all aridity and disenchantment
it is perennial as the grass.

Take kindly the counsel of the years,
gracefully surrendering the things of youth.

Nurture strength of spirit to shield you in sudden
   misfortune,
but do not distress yourself with imaginings.
Many fears are born of fatigue and loneliness.

Beyond wholesome discipline,
be gentle with yourself.

You are a child of the universe,
you have a right to be here.

Therefore be at peace with God,
whatever you conceive him to be,
and whatever your labors and aspirations,
in the noisy confusion of life keep peace with your
   soul.

With all its shame, drudgery, and broken dreams,
it is still a beautiful world.

Be cheerful.

Strive to be happy.

—MAX EHRMANN

NOTES

The abbreviation SE refers to the *Spiritual Exercises of St. Ignatius* (Translation and Commentary by George E. Ganss, S.J., Chicago: Loyola University Press, 1992).

"Stages of Life," by Herman Hesse is from *The Glass Bead Game* (Magister Ludi), translated by Richard and Clara Winston, New York: Henry Holt, An Owl Book, 1990, p.444.

Beatrix Kolk, O.S.B. was abbess of the Abbey of the Holy Cross in Herstelle, Germany from 1966 to 1994.

The Desiderata is often cited as having been "found in old Saint Paul's Church, Baltimore, dated 1692." The piece was in fact written in 1927 by Max Ehrmann, "The Sage of Terre Haute," Indiana.

Peter G. van Breemen, S.J. is the author of several books, including *The God Who Won't Let Go* (Ave Maria Press, 1991), *As Bread That Is Broken, Called by Name, Certain as the Dawn,* and *Let All God's Glory Through.* His influence on the church stretches worldwide, as his best-selling books have been published in many languages. He presently resides in Aachen, Germany, where he is a retreat director and spiritual director.

Other Titles in the
Ignatian Impulse Series

*These brief, readable, engaging
books present the spirituality of
St. Ignatius as a practical resource
for spiritual seekers of all faiths.*

The Art of Discernment
Making Good Decisions in Your World of Choices
Stefan Kiechle, S.J.
Anxiety, uncertainty, vulnerability—anyone who has
made a big decision knows these feelings. And as the
complexity of our decisions grows we seek
guidance in dealing with life's endless possibilities.
Stefan Kiechle offers a clear explanation of the
discernment process first developed by St. Ignatius of
Loyola and refined by his followers in the
centuries since.
ISBN: 1-59471-035-X / 128 pages / $9.95

The Sevenfold Yes
Affirming the Goodness of Our Deepest Desires
Willi Lambert, S.J.
At the heart of spirituality is a yes to life. *The
Sevenfold Yes*, an affirmation of life's goodness
and meaning, is at the very center of the
spirituality of St. Ignatius whose motto was to
"find God in all things." Practical prayer
exercises and insightful reflection questions help
readers to recognize God's call in the desires of
one's heart and in the events of everyday life.
ISBN: 1-59471-034-1 / 128 pages / $9.95

KEYCODE: F0A0105000